# CHILDREN'S ILLUSTRATORS

# PAUL O. ZELINSKY

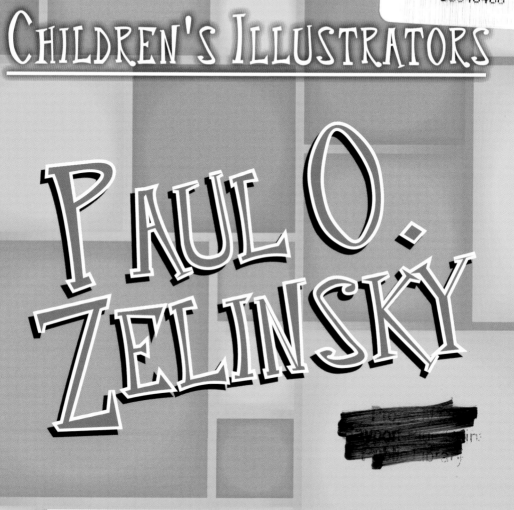

Sheila Griffin Llanas

**ABDO Publishing Company**

## visit us at
## www.abdopublishing.com

Published by ABDO Publishing Company, PO Box 398166, Minneapolis, MN 55439. Copyright © 2012 by Abdo Consulting Group, Inc. International copyrights reserved in all countries. No part of this book may be reproduced in any form without written permission from the publisher. The Checkerboard Library™ is a trademark and logo of ABDO Publishing Company.

Printed in the United States of America, North Mankato, Minnesota.
102011
012012

 PRINTED ON RECYCLED PAPER

Cover Photo: courtesy Paul O. Zelinsky
Interior Photos: courtesy Paul O. Zelinsky pp. 5, 6, 7, 11, 13, 19
  *Rumpelstiltskin* by Paul O. Zelinsky. Used by permission of Penguin Group (USA) Inc. All rights reserved. p. 9; *Rapunzel* by Paul O. Zelinsky. Used by permission of Penguin Group (USA) Inc. All rights reserved. p. 10; *The Maid and the Mouse and the Odd-Shaped House* by Paul O. Zelinsky. Used by permission of Penguin Group (USA) Inc. All rights reserved. p. 14; *Hansel and Gretel* by Rika Lesser, illustrated by Paul O. Zelinsky. Used by permission of Penguin Group (USA) Inc. All rights reserved. p. 15; *The Wheels On the Bus* by Paul O. Zelinsky. Used by permission of Penguin Group (USA) Inc. All rights reserved. p. 17; *Swamp Angel* by Anne Isaacs, illustrated by Paul O. Zelinsky. Used by permission of Penguin Group (USA) Inc. All rights reserved. p. 18; From *Knick-Knack Paddywhack* © 2002 by Paul O. Zelinsky. Used by permission of Dutton Children's Books, A Division of Penguin Young Readers Group, A Member of Penguin Group (USA) Inc. All rights reserved. p. 20

Series Coordinator: BreAnn Rumsch / Editors: Megan M. Gunderson, BreAnn Rumsch
Art Direction: Neil Klinepier

### Library of Congress Cataloging-in-Publication Data

Llanas, Sheila Griffin, 1958-
 Paul O. Zelinsky / Sheila Griffin Llanas.
   p. cm. -- (Children's illustrators)
 Includes index.
 ISBN 978-1-61783-250-5
 1. Zelinsky, Paul O.--Juvenile literature. 2. Illustrators--United States--Biography--Juvenile literature. I. Title.
 NC975.5.Z44L59 2012
 741.6'42092--dc23
   [B]
                              2011030806

# CONTENTS

# MAKING A MASTERPIECE

Paul O. Zelinsky once wrote, "I was born quite young, at about age zero." And in an interview he once said, "Forgetting things is one of my major talents." As you can see, Zelinsky has a great sense of humor! He also has a great career as a children's book illustrator.

Since 1978, Zelinsky has illustrated more than 30 books. His images often look like masterpieces. This is because he enjoys painting in the styles of the Italian **Renaissance**.

Yet since childhood, Zelinsky has loved the surprise of art. He sees each new story he illustrates in a **unique** way. So he does not stick to just one art style. That way, he gets to see paintings emerge that he did not expect!

*Zelinsky doesn't want his artwork to be limited by his known skills. That is why he lets the story tell him what kind of art to try next!*

# The Taste of Color

Paul O. Zelinsky was born in Evanston, Illinois, on February 14, 1953. His mother, Zelda, was a medical illustrator. His father, Daniel, was a math professor. Paul grew up with older sister Mara and younger brother David.

Paul's father taught at many different colleges. So, the family moved a lot. Paul was always the new kid at school. But, it never took long for his classmates to see he was an artist.

In addition to drawing, Paul loved to read. One of his favorite books was *The Story of Ferdinand* by Munro Leaf. He also liked Gustaf Tenggren's pictures in *The Tawny, Scrawny Lion.*

But it was another book that made a lasting impression on Paul. In *The Color Kittens* by Margaret Wise Brown, kittens mix paints and make new colors. This story gave Paul a feeling inside that was as strong as a flavor. Eventually, Paul would focus on this sense when creating his art for picture books.

*For a time, Paul's family lived in Japan. There, he drew pictures of geishas. These Japanese women wore traditional dresses called kimonos. One of Paul's drawings was printed in **Highlights** magazine!*

# CREATIVE KID

The Zelinsky family eventually settled in Wilmette, Illinois, where Paul grew up. During this time, Paul continued to **excel** at drawing. He filled his notebooks with doodles. He tried to keep these notebooks neat, but he could not stop drawing! Paul's classmates sometimes stood around his desk and watched him draw.

Paul's creativity extended beyond drawing. One year for Halloween, he dressed as a traffic light. He made the costume out of a big cardboard box. Paul held a flashlight inside the box to make its red, yellow, and green light lenses glow. The red one said "trick or treat" and the green one said "thank you"!

Paul also liked acting. When he was 11, Paul starred in the play *Rumpelstiltskin* at the Wilmette Children's Theater. He played the title role of the dwarf who spun straw into gold.

In high school, Paul continued to create art. He illustrated poems his friends wrote and stories he read in English class. In art classes, he learned many new skills. He especially enjoyed printmaking.

Around this time, one of Paul's sketches was published in a math textbook. Yet, he wasn't thinking about becoming an illustrator. Instead, he imagined becoming an astronomer, an **architect**, or a **taxidermist**.

*As a adult, Paul remained fascinated by the mischievous Rumpelstiltskin. He published a beautiful version of the story in 1986.*

# WORLD OF POSSIBILITY

After graduating from high school, Paul studied art at Yale University in New Haven, Connecticut. During his second year, he took a class about picture books. One of the teachers was children's author Maurice Sendak. Paul found Sendak to be warm and funny. As Paul learned about picture books, something clicked. He thought, "I could do this."

Paul began working toward this new goal. One of his classmates liked to write. So together, they wrote and illustrated several children's stories and sent them to publishers. One story was accepted for publication. Yet before the book could be printed, the company closed.

*Zelinsky's 1997 book,* **Rapunzel,** *features many details inspired by his time in Italy. These include historic buildings and the styles and techniques of Renaissance art.*

In 1974, Paul earned his **degree** from Yale and decided to earn another. So, he attended the Tyler School of Art at Temple University in Philadelphia, Pennsylvania.

Tyler's art program offered students an opportunity to spend one year in Rome, Italy. There, Paul studied Italian art from the **Medieval**, **Renaissance**, and **Baroque** periods. From those beautiful styles, Paul learned many new art **techniques**.

*In Rome, Zelinsky lived and worked in a villa near the Tiber River.*

# CHANGE OF PACE

In 1976, Zelinsky earned his master's **degree** in fine arts from Temple. He decided to become an art teacher. Zelinsky found a position teaching art in California. Yet there was one big problem. Zelinsky did not love this job. He also realized that teaching was not his best skill.

Zelinsky remembered Sendak's class at Yale and how much he had enjoyed illustrating stories. Deep down, he knew children's book illustration was the right career for him.

So in 1977, Zelinsky moved to Brooklyn Heights in New York City, New York. At first, he earned money illustrating magazine and newspaper articles. Meanwhile, he visited publishing houses and showed his **portfolio** to children's book editors.

Finally, an editor asked Zelinsky to illustrate a book by well-known children's author Avi. The book was called *Emily Upham's Revenge, or How Deadwood Dick Saved the Banker's*

*Zelinsky once said, "I want to make pictures that speak in the same voice as the words."*

*Niece, a Massachusetts Adventure.* Zelinsky had to figure out how to fit all those words on the book's cover!

Next, Zelinsky illustrated *How I Hunted the Little Fellows*, a Russian story by Boris Zhitkov. And in 1980, he illustrated another book by Avi called *The History of Helpless Harry*. It seemed that Zelinsky had finally found a good fit.

# FAMILY AND FAIRY TALES

While in New York, Zelinsky fell in love with a woman named Deborah Hallen. She was a pianist and an elementary school teacher. The couple married in 1981 and later had two daughters named Anna and Rachel.

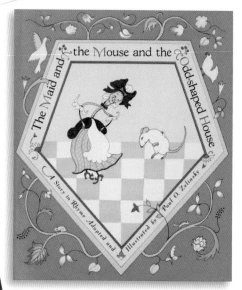

**The Maid and the Mouse and the Odd-shaped House**

The year he married, Paul also wrote his first book. It is called *The Maid and the Mouse and the Odd-shaped House.* He created drawings with thin lines and painted them with pale colors. These illustrations set a playful tone for the **rhyming** text.

In 1984, Zelinsky felt inspired to illustrate the Brothers Grimm fairy tale *Hansel and Gretel.* He asked his friend Rika Lesser to write a new version of

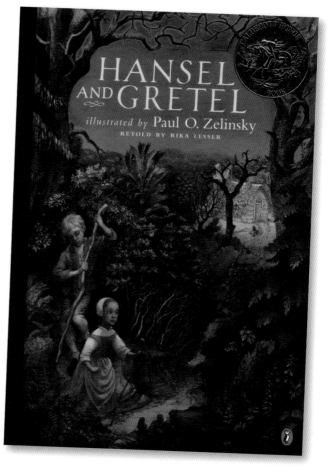

the story. To research his artwork, Zelinsky visited the Metropolitan Museum of Art in New York City. There, he studied Dutch art from the 1600s. He also spent time walking in the woods. He imagined how it would feel to be lost, like Hansel and Gretel had been.

With his research complete, Zelinsky got to work using some of the **techniques** he had learned in Italy. He started by taking his watercolors and making an underpainting all in grays called a **grisaille**. Then he sealed the paper.

Finally, he added layer after layer of transparent, colorful oil paints. This detailed work paid off. The next year, *Hansel and Gretel* was named a **Caldecott Honor Book**.

# A Colorful Career

Zelinsky's big success brought more opportunity. He next illustrated *The Story of Mrs. Lovewright and Purrless Her Cat* by Lore Segal. During this project, he remembered reading Brown's *The Color Kittens* long ago and sensing colors as flavors.

Segal's funny tale seemed tangy to Paul. So as he painted, he thought about dill pickles. He tried to create pictures that looked the way pickles taste! The book was published in 1985.

The next year, Zelinsky returned to fairy tales. He adapted and illustrated *Rumpelstiltskin*, another Brothers Grimm story. Using the same **technique** as in *Hansel and Gretel*, Zelinsky created detailed oil paintings that looked like richly colored **Renaissance** artwork. In 1987, the book earned Zelinsky his second **Caldecott Honor**.

Not long after, Zelinsky decided to make a different kind of picture book. He heard the song "The Wheels on the Bus" for the first time and imagined it as a moving-parts book. Zelinsky got to

The WHEELS on the BUS
A BOOK WITH
MOVABLE
PARTS
ORANGE ST.
ADAPTED & ILLUST
PAUL O. ZEL

***The 1990 book became incredibly popular, selling millions of copies.***

work. He made the bus's wheels spin, its doors open, and the passengers bounce in their seats! Children everywhere loved *The Wheels on the Bus*. Today, it remains one of Zelinsky's most popular titles.

## ELEMENTS OF ART: COLOR

Color is one of the basic parts of art. Objects have color because they reflect or absorb light. The lightness or darkness of a color is called its value or tone.

Zelinsky uses many colors in his books. In fact, he loves color so much that his favorite changes every day! Depending on the story, Zelinsky may select bright colors or rich colors. He often uses oil paints. This allows him to use color to create depth and the effects of light and shadow.

# ULTIMATE REWARD

Once again, Zelinsky's next project took his art in a new direction. *Swamp Angel* by Anne Isaacs tells the story of Angelica Longrider, the greatest woodswoman in Tennessee.

Zelinsky thought a folk-art style would work best for this tall tale set in the Tennessee wilds. Instead of paper, he painted on thin **veneer** made from cedar and aspen wood. The wood was challenging to work with. But Zelinsky liked how the wood's **grain** framed his paintings. In 1995, *Swamp Angel* earned him his third **Caldecott Honor**.

*Zelinsky's art combines elements of fantasy and reality.*

**Dust Devil** *features the same beautiful wood veneers as* **Swamp Angel.**

For the next several years, Zelinsky worked on his own retelling of the Brothers Grimm tale *Rapunzel*. He conducted a lot of research about the story's background. He also used models to help him draw realistic people. He studied them sitting, standing, and moving. His daughter Rachel even inspired his young Rapunzel.

Zelinsky returned to the **Renaissance** style for the artwork in *Rapunzel*. It gave the book a classic feel. Finally in 1997, the book was published. His years of work turned out to be worth it. After three honor books, *Rapunzel* finally earned the 1998 **Caldecott Medal**.

# INSPIRED IN BROOKLYN

In 2002, Zelinsky published his second moving-parts book. *Knick-Knack Paddywhack* is a pop-up version of the silly counting song "This Old Man." The book took more than a year to create. It was named one of the New York Times' Best

Illustrated Books of the Year. It was the first moving-parts book to earn this award.

Since then, Zelinsky has continued to illustrate popular picture books. These include *Toys Go Out* by Emily Jenkins and *Awful Ogre Running Wild* by Jack Prelutsky. Zelinsky also revisited the folk-art world of Angelica Longrider for Anne Isaacs's *Dust Devil*. This 2010 **sequel** to *Swamp Angel* tells a tall tale about Angelica's giant horse.

Today, Zelinsky still lives in Brooklyn with his wife. They like to stroll along the Brooklyn Heights Promenade. From there, they can see the Statue of Liberty, the Brooklyn Bridge, and the skyline of Lower Manhattan.

Zelinsky spends his days in his art studio, just a few short blocks from home. There, his drawing table sits under a large window facing a churchyard. As he works, Zelinsky remembers the pleasure of story and color he learned from Brown's *The Color Kittens*. Today, his art gives the same joy to many young readers. Zelinsky feels lucky to have found such a fun career.

*Each copy of* **Knick-Knack Paddywhack** *takes 50 people more than one hour to assemble!*

# GLOSSARY

**architect** - a person who plans and designs buildings. His or her work is called architecture.

**Baroque** (buh-ROHK) - of, relating to, or having the characteristics of an artistic style from the 1600s. It is marked by the use of complex forms and bold ornamentation, which create a sense of drama.

**Caldecott Honor Book** - a runner-up to the Caldecott Medal. The Caldecott Medal is an award the American Library Association gives to the artist who illustrated the year's best picture book.

**degree** - a title given by a college to its students for completing their studies.

**excel** - to be better than others.

**grain** - the way the lines or fibers in something, such as wood, are arranged.

**grisaille** (grih-ZEYE) - decoration in tones of a single color, especially gray, designed to produce a three-dimensional effect.

**Medieval** (mee-DEE-vuhl) - of or belonging to the Middle Ages. The Middle Ages was a period in European history from about AD 500 to 1500.

**portfolio** - a selection of work, especially of drawings, paintings, or photographs. It may be presented to show one's skill as an artist.

**Renaissance** (reh-nuh-SAHNS) - a cultural movement that began in Italy during the 1300s. It was expressed through art, literature, and the beginnings of modern science.

**rhyme** - words or lines ending with similar sounds.

**sequel** - a book, movie, or other work that continues the story begun in a preceding one.

**taxidermist** - someone who prepares, stuffs, and mounts the skins of dead animals so that they look like they did when they were alive.

**technique** - a method or style in which something is done.

**unique** - being the only one of its kind.

**veneer** (vuh-NIHR) - a thin sheet of a material, as in wood.

# WEB SITES

To learn more about Paul O. Zelinsky, visit ABDO Publishing Company online. Web sites about Paul O. Zelinsky are featured on our Book Links page. These links are routinely monitored and updated to provide the most current information available.

**www.abdopublishing.com**

# INDEX